Other Shepherds

Other Shepherds

Nina Kossman

poems with translations from
Marina Tsvetaeva

Some of these poems and translations first appeared in *Columbia*, *The American Voice*, *Live Encounters*, *The Antioch Review*, *Unlikely Stories*, *The Connecticut Poetry Review*, *Eurolitnetwork.com* / *Trafika Europe*, *The Virginia Quarterly Review*, *Latitude on 2nd*, *Empirical*, *When Women Waken*, *Raddle Moon*, *Artful Dodge*, *Prism International*, *The Antigonish Review*, *Poet Lore*, *Prairie Schooner*. In addition, some of these translations appeared in *Marina Tsvetaeva: Poem of the End: Selected Narrative and Lyrical Poems*, translated by Nina Kossman, published by Ardis in 1998, reprinted by Overlook Press in 2004, and currently out of print.

Cover image: Nina Kossman

Published 2020 in New York by Poets & Traitors Press
www.poets-traitors.com
poetstraitors@gmail.com

Editors: Val Vinokur, Olga Livshin, Julia Curl

Published in the United States of America.

Poets & Traitors Press is an independent publisher of books of poetry and translations by a single author/translator. The press emerged from the Poet/Translator Reading Series and from the New School's Literary Translation Workshop to showcase authors who travel between writing and translation, artists for whom Language is made manifest through languages and whose own word carries, shapes, and is shaped by that of another.

Poets & Traitors Press acknowledges support from Eugene Lang College, the New School Bachelor's Program for Adults and Transfer Students, and the New School Foreign Languages Department.

ISBN: 978-0-9990737-4-2

In memory of my parents and my brother.

Other Shepherds

CONTENTS

CONTENTS

PREFACE

The art you see on the front cover of this book is a little watercolor I made at the age of six. In the early and mid-seventies, those who had been fortunate to be granted permission to emigrate from the Soviet Union were not allowed to take out anything that could be considered national patrimony: art, icons, antiquities, certain manuscripts, and books published before 1917. Sometimes these items could be smuggled out in diplomatic pouches. But there were no diplomatic relations between the Soviet Union and Israel—the only country to which Soviet Jews were allowed to apply for permission to immigrate to in those years. Instead, the Dutch Embassy served as a kind of an intermediary, accepting art, books, and documents from emigrants in Moscow and returning them upon their owners' arrival in Israel. But there was a limit to how many items the Dutch Consul would take. My parents had to choose between my pictures and my mother's dissertation. I told my parents that I wouldn't leave without my pictures. And so my mother's dissertation on nucleic acids was left behind in our empty apartment. Hopefully, a copy of it can still be found in the Lenin Library in Moscow. Such is the provenance of the little watercolor on the front cover.

I must have been attached to that landscape picture as a tangible trace of origin. But if it were possible to have a graph of personal development that reflected intangible things—or rather not things but states of the soul, alienation, and nostalgia resulting in a kind of personal rebirth—then I would say that Tsvetaeva's poems acted as a kind of midwife. I first read them in Cleveland at the end of my childhood in January 1974, and they helped deliver me from that dark night of the soul into something livable. A kind of moldable model of existence that I have followed for the rest of my life—up to this very moment.

Cleveland was where my family—my parents, my brother, and I—spent our first year in America. I mention alienation and nostalgia because reading Tsvetaeva for the first time helped me deal with these two intangibles. It would be trite to say she "inspired me," but perhaps by demonstrating that these intangibles can ruin you if you give in to them without resistance, she also showed they could be the fodder for poems. Thus, the cocktail of nostalgia, alienation, and immersion in Tsvetaeva resulted in my own first poems, and as I was still well-rooted in my native language, those poems were in Russian. Sometimes I ask myself: Why was I writing poems in Russian while, in the outside world, I was totally immersed in English? I think the answer lies in the words "the outside world." The ways of nostalgia and alienation are strange, perhaps just as strange as the ways we choose to deal with them. For the first few years of my American life, I had no interest in writing poems in English, precisely because English was the language I had to use in the outside world—at school, in the city, etc. Instead, my poems sprang from the interior world, and at that age I resisted the outside world and created—possibly at the expense of a comfortable co-existence with my peers—a world of my own. Here, my past and my present, so different in real life, were one. In my mid-20s, I returned to Tsvetaeva. This time not only as a reader and a fan but as a translator. Translating Tsvetaeva was yet another attempt at bridging, within myself, two disparate interior worlds, not to mention languages and cultures. In the 1990s, I had two books of my own poems published. *Pereboi* ("Syncopated Rhythms") was published in Moscow, one year before the fall of the Soviet Union, and *Po pravuyi ruku sna* ("To the Right of a Dream") in the US. Once in a while, I refer to them as bilingual, while in fact, there were more poems in Russian in those two books than in English.

I'd like to say a few words about the title of this book. Other

Shepherds comes from my translation of Tsvetaeva's poem which ends with, "There is an island—thank God!— / Where I don't need a tambourine, / Where black wool / Hangs from every fence. Yes / —There are in the world black flocks, / Other shepherds." (1920). Although the poem's protagonist is addressing a lover, I took the last line slightly out of its amorous context and used it in a broader sense, in a kind of social, or rather, existential sense. I don't believe that I have sinned against the poet by looking at her poem this way; in fact, I think the poem is quite amenable to this interpretation, especially if we look at the ending of the penultimate stanza. "In your flock there was no / Sheep blacker than I") which resonates far beyond the personal context of a rejected woman speaking to her lover.

I was born in the same Communist dystopia that, a few decades before my birth, led Marina Tsvetaeva to hang herself. This was a place where "being different," an uncomfortable feeling in any society at any time, led to much more than the usual social ostracism; where comrades were clearly divided into "white sheep" and "black sheep," and where the black sheep didn't end up very well. Leaving the Soviet Union as a child, my experience of "black-sheep-ness" was somewhat limited, but I have been very aware of my parents' experience, particularly that of my mother—a Jew, a daughter of an "enemy of the people," a student of genetics in the era of Lysenko (the official Soviet biologist who rejected genetics), and thus thrice an outsider in a society that didn't tolerate outsiders.

The title has another meaning too. Having lived in two so-called "superpowers," i.e. having spent my childhood in the Soviet Union, where personal freedoms were curtailed, and my youth and adulthood in "something of its opposite" (my way of referring to the US as a teenager) with its seemingly unlimited personal freedoms, I found both wanting. Being a "black sheep" in the Soviet Union was not only painful psychologically. It pushed you to the edge of a very real abyss, since a threat of physical extermination was real. In the US, being a black sheep in a herd, a society where outsiders are accepted, yields only psychological pain. And so an immigrant from the former Soviet Union swings between these two. These are two very different kinds of "black-sheep-ness," one hard core and the other soft. The black sheep consciousness continues in the so-called free world, attenuated, without the attendant fear of physical extermination.

As for "other" in the title, it goes without saying that in my childhood I lived in a country that wasn't shepherded well, or rather, whose Chief Shepherd was incapable of fulfilling his husbandry without shackling or hobbling his sheep. Since my family and I arrived in the US during the Watergate fiasco, it goes without saying that the then US president was not a good shepherd either. Yet, in those years, my new country, the US, was still a functioning democracy, and it remains to be seen whether it will survive the current COVID-19 crisis and its current shepherd-in-chief, to reemerge, once again, as a democracy.

In Greek mythology, the image of a king or a prince often blends in with that of a shepherd. Paris, one of Priam's sons, is the most well-known example. Some of the poems in this collection observe the lives of mythical characters and ask one to imagine what it would be like to be ruled by other shepherds, philosopher-kings ideally suited to govern.

A few words about the structure of this book. I braided together my Tsvetaeva translations and my own English poems mostly by theme, especially when my poem seemed to echo a motif in Tsvetaeva's. Although my poems were not written with Tsvetaeva's work in mind, I found quite a few that can be seen as my responses to her.

For example, Tsvetaeva's poem, written in 1918, begins with "My light tread" and ends with "God placed me alone /In the midst of the great world.—You are not a woman but a bird, / So, then—fly and sing." While in Tsvetaeva's poem, it is God who speaks, telling her of her bird destiny, in my matching poem, it is a man—not God—who assumes the authority, if not the right, to proclaim the female protagonist of the poem "a queen of birds, / a swallow with a woman's face and a swallow's soul..." In Tsvetaeva's poem, we are not told whether the speaker of the poem—the poet—agrees with God on the subject of the role He assigns her. Perhaps she does, perhaps she does not. In my poem, the woman clearly does not agree with the man, yet at the end, she is transformed into a bird against her wishes: "She was so overcome with the sadness of it all, / that she opened her mouth to say, "You're so wrong!" / But only bird sounds issued from her throat." Thus, although these two poems, written a hundred years apart, arrive at the same image ("woman as bird") from completely different ways of thinking, at some point, they come together. It is a strange togetherness, or perhaps, a strange parting of the ways, and because clearly a parting presupposes a meeting, it is a kind of broken-up togetherness. Here's another pair. Speaking to the goddess of love in "Praise to Aphrodite (IV)," Tsvetaeva sees the world of mortals as totally subjected to the goddess ("Mortal whitewater, salt of the sea... / In whitewater and torture, /How long are we to heed your call / O armless sculpture?"). In my matching poem ("Snow-cooled, / rain-soaked") people are indifferent to gods ("in the grove of the gods / who no longer rule us."). Indeed, a hundred years after Tsvetaeva wrote, "Still, the deadly sweat overflows / Your golden bowl," we can say with some certainty that, for better or for worse, we are not ruled by the ancient gods, not even the gods of love and temptation.

We see a very different goddess in Tsvetaeva's 1921 poem, "From the Mind's Dreams." This time, the goddess is not a familiar deity from Greek mythology. In fact, she is not from any known mythology. She is Tsvetaeva's own goddess, and her name in this poem is simply "Goddess of Faithfulness." This poem is one of the most intense in Tsvetaeva's oeuvre, and it's one of those few translations in which I preserved the rhythm and rhyme pattern of the original completely. The poem is nothing less than a supplication to the Goddess ("As safe as bone encased in a grave, / Goddess of Faithfulness, keep your slave") who, by demanding total obedience, leads the speaker to suffering and finally to death ("Her ribs to the post, with your sharpest stave, / Goddess of Faithfulness, now stab your slave!"). In my poem ("Love is a motionless goddess"), the goddess no longer demands anything; in fact, this 21st century goddess of love seems to practice Zen: "The goddess of love is so still / That even the sun is paralyzed." She expects nothing, she wants nothing: "She will look at the stone forever. / Her eyes are open. Its eyes are shut." She is not going to make anyone suffer or die in a horrific way; she is truly a Zen goddess of love. She is motionless, looking at nothing, desiring nothing.

Something else is born of this strange pairing, a kind of tense new world. I place my poems beside Tsvetaeva's not in competition but with humility. The aim is not to emulate her but to create a dialogue between her poem and mine, a resonance possible not only between two poets but between two eras. My goal is not to aspire to her heights, which are unscalable, as they are hers and no one else's, but to approach her and to speak.

—Nina Kossman

Other Shepherds

I remember the first day, the infantile brutality,
The languor and the divine dregs of a swallow.
The carelessness of the hands, the heartlessness of the heart
Falling like a stone—and like a hawk—onto my chest.

And now—trembling from heat and pity, what's left
Is this: to howl like a wolf, this: to fall at your feet,
To lower my eyes, knowing the penalty for pleasure—
A convict's passion and a cruel love.

M.T. (1917)

You, who are lost,
who were you then,
when time stood still
like a hollow rock,
where can you find it,
in what far-flung night?
You said it was yours,
time was your god, you said,
or did you want to say
that you were its servant?
But now it has abandoned you—
you are a withered king
on a solitary throne
"She is my love, my bride, my very own..."
Ah, but where is she now,
your queen, your soul?
In the ground she lies,
in a wooden coffin,
under a heavy stone.

N.K.

From your arrogant Poland
You brought me flattering words,
And a sable hat,
And your hand with long fingers,
And bows, and endearments,
And a princely coat-of-arms with a crown.

—But I brought you
Two silver wings.

M.T. (1917)

Words for wings, less for more,
as sea is for мope*,
red for white,
sweet for dry,
petals for a flower,
a flower as a gift:
something that wilts
for something that lasts,
something that passes
for something that stays...
Repeat: mirror for memory—
I shan't accept this gift.

N.K.

* *мope - sea (Russian)*

(In Memory of Béranger)

A bad mother!—My ill fame
Grows and blossoms every day.
First the Sly One takes me to a feast,
Then my first-born's forgotten for a quill...

Envying the empresses of fashion,
And the little dancer in her tights,
Over the crib I watch the years run by,
Not seeing that my milk is running out!

And which of you, hypocrites,
Didn't feast then and forget to pay!
I swear by the bottle of my patron
As I swore by yours once—Béranger!

But to one—through storms and delights—
Though fickle, I'm faithful still:
Make no mistake, my ill fame:
—A bad mother but a faithful wife!

M.T. (1918)

Flesh of my flesh,
hollow tomb-child,
away, you carnival of dreamed up shallows!
Warmth returning,
reluctant idol—
out of the beating of my heart and sense!

Bliss of my bliss,
sleep of the future,
come close, speak softly, be my guest,
watch waves of feeling
fold back into face,
fold upon fold—unwanted infants.

Row upon row—ungrateful torsos:
giving them life is not worth the trouble.
They will tear apart
placenta,
red,
they will feed off my generous handfuls.

Ghastly babies, like balding beasts,
like cubs of flowers that grab and wail,
the more you watch them the louder they cry—
idols their eyes,
gods their bodies,
their cribs—mausoleums of sin.

Ripple your own waters.
Rip off your own past.
Meek, weak, or plain gloomy,
swim in your own pus.

Sullen reflections
of hostile faces—

Flesh of my flesh?
No.
Eye for an eye.
And tooth.

                                        N.K.

My light tread
—A sign of clear conscience—
My light tread,
My ringing song—

God placed me alone
In the midst of the great world.
—You are not a woman but a bird,
So, then—fly and sing.

M.T. (1918)

"Denial won't help," he said in a harsh voice.
"Denial of your bird nature," he explained a bit more kindly,
while she whose bird nature was thus discussed
neither flew nor spoke but gazed straight ahead,
and there were no trees and no sky in what she saw,
only a wall, a barrier that could break her:
she was not a bird, after all, only a woman
made of skin and blood and human tissue,
and her bird nature existed only in his far-flung words.
That's what she was thinking as she stood there,
her eyes on the wall, listening to him,
as he was proclaiming her a queen of birds,
a swallow with a woman's face and a swallow's soul,
that, with her swallow's wings and a swallow's tail,
could fly high above the boredom of the mundane.
She was so overcome with the sadness of it all,
that she opened her mouth to say, "You're so wrong!"
But only bird sounds issued from her throat.

N.K.

I am not an impostor, for I came home.
I am not a maid: I do not ask for bread.
I am your passion, your Sunday rest,
Your seventh day, your seventh heaven.
There, on earth, they gave me nothing
And hung millstones around my neck.
—Don't you recognize me, beloved?
I am your swallow: Psyche.

M.T. (1918)

PSYCHE

I evoke you but you're asleep.
I awaken you but you don't hear.
Your sleeping breath reaches from here to there
In a majestic arc thrown from shore to shore.
When I'm near you, I'm near an ocean:
Voices, wave-like, break their will to the ear
Of the mind that only seems asleep.
The intelligence of sleep you've given me,
the goodness of thought that comes from
                    a deeper peace,
from under the static rippling the surface.
To still the surface, I evoke you.

N.K.

Words are inscribed in the black sky,
And the beautiful eyes go blind...
And the deathbed is no longer terrible,
And the love bed is no longer sweet.

Sweat from writing—sweat from ploughing.
We know another ardor:
Weightless fire dancing around the curls—
The breeze of inspiration.

M.T. (1918)

HOW TO BRING A DEAD SONG TO LIFE

Even within her heart
the song didn't break
the song kept her heart
just as the heart kept the song
she forgot its words
but the tune remained
sheltered inside her
so deep
she thought it was gone
so deep
she thought it had left her
she couldn't reach it
it hid beneath the snow
inside her heart
and when the snow melted
it revealed a skeleton
shriveled bones

The song was dead

How do you bring a dead song to life?
A dead song has more power
a dead song twisted inside you
how do you live with so much death?
death outside her
death inside her
one outweighed the other
she breathed life into the one inside her
and when the song matured
it left her
as a grown child leaves Mother
and she was left alone again
mute
for the rest of her life.

N.K.

Bring to me all that's no use to others:
My fire must burn it all!
I lure life, and I lure death
As weightless gifts to my fire.

Fire loves light-weighted things:
Last year's brushwood, wreathes, words.
Fire blazes from this kind of food.
You will rise from it purer than ash!

I am the Phoenix; only in the fire do I sing.
Provide for my miraculous life!
I burn high—and I burn to the ground.
From now on let your nights be light-filled.

The icy fire—the fiery fount.
I hold high my tall form,
I hold high my high rank
Of Confidante and Heiress!

M.T. (1918)

You are a force
deep inside me
that doesn't know my name.

(See me throw it into the fire.)

That, deaf to my entreaties,
wouldn't rescue me
from a burning house.

(See me throw it into the sea.)

That wouldn't save me
if I were drowning.
And if I drowned, it would drown too.

(See me throw it into a forest.)

That wouldn't look for me
if I were lost in a forest.
(If I were lost, it would be lost with me.)

See me throw it back into me:

How you dissolve, how you melt away,
no longer a force,
just a dead man's soul.

                                        N.K.

(to P. Antokolsky)

I give you a present, an iron ring:
Insomnia—ecstasy—and hopelessness.
So that you won't look girls in the face,
So that you'll forget even the word tenderness.

So that you'll lift your head, with its errant curls,
Like a frothy goblet, into space,
So that this iron ornament will turn
Into coal—into dust—into ashes.

When to your soothsayer's curls
Love itself clings, like a red-hot coal,
Then be silent and press to your lips
The iron ring on your dark finger.
Here's a talisman against red lips,
Here's the first link in your chain armor—
So that you'll stand alone in the storm of days,
Like an oak—like God in his iron circle!

M.T. (March 1919)

I brought you a gift
the green of chestnuts
the white of carnations
the blue of the sea
which you shall not sail
the chestnuts have fallen
the carnations have wilted
the sea is a postcard
which you threw away

                                        N.K.

I am happy to live impeccably and simply
Like a calendar—a pendulum—like the sun.
A worldly recluse of shapely size,
As wise as any creature of God.

To know: spirit is my helpmate, and spirit—my guide.
To enter without a word, like a ray and a look.
To live as I write: tersely, impeccably—
The way God commanded and friends don't approve.

M.T. *(1919)*

I would give up
everything
everyone
everywhere
values more than anything
a job
a house
a man
a settled life
but I would not give up
the first stirrings of a poem
a word that becomes a story
a painting that asks to be born
a child of the soul of my flesh
therefore
I cannot give up
the way of life that makes
a poem
a story
a painting
possible

N.K.

It smelled of England—and the sea—
And valor.—He's harsh and slender.
—So, binding myself to a new grief,
I laugh, as a ship's boy in the rigging

Laughs during a big storm,
Alone with the Lord's wrath,
In a blissful, ape-like folly,
Dancing over the foaming maw.
—These hands are stubborn—the rigging's
Firm,—it's used to storms at sea!
And the heart is valiant—even so,
Not everyone will die in bed!

Inhaling the cold of the starless
Dark,—on the mast itself—on the edge—
Over the gaping chasm
—Laughing!—I lower my eyes...

M.T. (1920)

Forever and ever,
fight upon flight,
sea waves upon seamen,
seaweed upon sunken trunks,
and a cry above it all—
gods of all nations, deliver us!
gods of all seas, unite!
Hero, so un-god-like,
goddess, so un-womanly,
upon a wave, so unworldly,
seas of all continents,
seas of all dreams,
those who fought you,
those who lived by you
now lie in your depths;
their arms are corals,
their hair is seaweed,
their dreams of reaching the shore
are nothing but sea water,
wave upon wave,
gods of all seas,
preserve the coral reefs
that used to be men.

N.K.

EARTHLY NAME

When parched with thirst, give me water,
One glass, or else I'll die.
Persistently—languidly—melodically—
I pledge my feverish cry

Repeated at length—yet still more fiercely,
Once more—again—
Tossing all night long for sleep,
Aware all sleep is spent.

As if the fields were not abounding
In herbs that grant relief.
Persistently—senselessly—redundantly—
An infant's babble repeats...

Thus, each utterance more final:
Noose—at the neck joint...
And if it's but an earthly name I'm moaning—
That's not the point.

M.T. (1920)

A NAME

A name shaped like a firebrand
a flower shaped like an eye
childhood of my memory
in the absolutely closed sky

a word shaped like a mouth-lid
a thought twisted from light
ruses of final solitude
fading in the final white

a mouth shaped into music
Ave Maria, reply!
help us shape our ecstasy
as we shape your drawn-out sigh

N.K.

To you, who bid farewell to love—
Farewell to you.
I had your fill of your offences.
I read in your eyes,
Like a scathing Biblical Psalm,
"The evil passion!"

In the hands that bring you food
You read flattery.
My laughter—O jealousy of other hearts!—
Grates on your ears
Like a tambourine of lepers.

From the way you grasp your pick
In your hands—so as not to touch
Mine (are not hands also flowers?)
It is as clear to me as night
That in your flock there was no
Sheep blacker than I.

There is an island—thank God!—
Where I don't need a tambourine,
Where black wool
Hangs from every fence. Yes—
There are in the world black flocks,
Other shepherds.

                                        M.T. (1920)

To speak of love
you have to know
what-is-love
what-love-is
whichever way you arrange the words,
it won't convince me

if you take what you need
and reject what you don't;
what sort of creature
is this "crown of creation"
who takes this
but rejects that
when love is offered
on a hand
like seeds
for birds
like feed
for sheep
to be slaughtered soon thereafter?
Should I follow the sheep
to the slaughterhouse
to end up
a carcass hung from a hook?
What need of a love
that uses me
like sheep
for wool
and mutton
and throws out what can't be used?
Cruelty of the shepherd
for whom "use"
is an axiom.
that needs no proof.
Nay,
I'm no sheep
destined for slaughter
nor a follower
of a shepherd
who kills
what he claims to love.

N.K.

Nailed to the pillory of shame
Of the ancient conscience of the Slavs,
Snake in my heart, stigma on my brow,
I still maintain that I am innocent.

I still insist that I share the peace
Of the pious receiving the Eucharist,
That it is not my fault my hand
Is held out in the streets for happiness.

Sort out all this trash,
Tell me—or am I blind?—
Where is my gold? Or my silver?
There are only ashes in my hand.

And this is all, with flattery and prayer,
I have received from those who are so happy.
And this is all that I will carry
Into the land of silent kisses.

M.T. (1920)

When the beautiful virgin was chosen for sacrifice
and hundreds of eyes were watching her,
the crystalline lens of her eye beheld
the whole gleaming horizon.
And when, dying, the virgin prayed
for a flock of angels
to coo around her body,
the people cried, "You witch, you filth!"
Her terrible end had been prophesied by an elder
from Babylon who traded in the evil eye;
he could see it all, he knew well how the firmament blazed.

—From the mass of Jewish deaths
may this virgin be resurrected,
may the Slavic murk blaze in her eyes,
add to that a handful of foreign anger
and, to pull her soul out of her body,
feed the people a tale about a foreign yoke!

She burned so brightly that, throwing back their heads,
the people stood and watched
as the fire swallowed her flesh.
And her soul could see the uninhabited shore
so vast, it could not be contained in the smallness of her eye
and when, satisfied with the spectacle,
the people had finally dispersed,
an angel carried her ashes away
to a bank of an underground river
where the ice never melts.

N.K.

With such force has her hand grasped
Her chin that her mouth twists in pain.
With such vividness envisioned the parting
That not even death may part them:

That is how a flag-bearer abandons his standard;
That is how a mother at the scaffold hears: Now!
That is how a concubine of the last monarch
Stares into the night with her last eyes.

M.T. (11 October 1921)

Stone words hard to wield,
smooth as the moon washed of night,
shape me into a weapon no man can see
except with the eyes of his bones.
Words tight as skin in a fleshless space,
worn thin in the cage of a promise,
design fast the leap into the air
no man can follow, see nor stop
with the frightened silk of nightly kisses
or daily prayers in his expectant hand.

N.K.

The gods are no longer generous
On the shore of this other river.
Doves of Venus, fly into
The sunset's wide gates.

Lying on cold sand,
I'll pass onto a day unmarked on the calendar...
Like a snake looking down on its cold skin,
I have outlived my youth.

M.T. (1921)

Lilies and Phoenician wine,
a loaf of coarse bread,
a simple shelter from the rain,
these are all you need,
so the light of Aldebaran
doesn't blind you before you are ready,
before you learn all the ways
in which your fate is welded to the stars
to make forgotten predictions come true,
only then will the lilies and the Phoenician wine
and the moon-colored poppies
rise like stars to the sky
which remembers names you've forgotten.

N.K.

PRAISE TO APHRODITE (IV)

How many of them feed off your hands,
White doves and gray doves!
Entire kingdoms coo and dance
Round your lips, Baseness!

Still, the deadly sweat overflows
Your golden bowl.
Even the crested warrior clings
Like a white she-dove.

On an evil day each cloud
Grows as round as breasts.
Every innocent flower
Bears your face, Temptress!

Mortal whitewater, salt of the sea...
In whitewater and torture,
How long are we to heed your call
O armless sculpture?

M.T. (1921)

Snow-cooled,
rain-soaked,
angered by stillness,
as though it were a crime,
eyes half-closed,
hands separating
anemones from asphodels,
stalk by stalk,
petal by petal...
And don't forget water-grass,
how it fed on the asphodel,
flower of the dead,
symbol of memory,
and that short burst of the sun
in the valley of the soon-to-be-dead,
while your tense hands
go on separating
petal from stalk,
oblivion from memory
in the grove of the gods
who no longer rule us.

N.K.

From the mind's dreams, from the bile's rage,
Goddess of Faithfulness, keep your slave.

With cast-iron hoops bind tight her breast,
Goddess of Faithfulness, be her nest.

Remove from the shrub all flowers and pips,
Make her mouth numb, then seal her lips.

As safe as bone encased in a grave,
Goddess of Faithfulness, keep your slave.

To keep your loom humming without a stop,
Her lips must learn the law of the lock.

Her ribs to the post, with your sharpest stave,
Goddess of Faithfulness, stab your slave!

M.T. (1921)

Love is a motionless goddess
Studying the eyes of a stone:
How long will they remain shut.

The stone is earth, and the wind,
Whirling it, knows its broken name:
Bones in motion spell out one dark caress,

While the goddess of love is so still
That even the sun is paralyzed
And the wind drops down its rushing arms;

The morning will never arrive,
Entangled in wings of the goddess.
Night is a river but the stone has no eyes

To plunge into love—
Unaware that a red boat of safety
Is rocking on black waves.

The goddess folds her narrow wings.
She will look at the stone forever.
Her eyes are open. Its eyes are shut.

N.K.

You wanted this. So. Alleluia.
I kiss the hand that strikes me.

I pull to my breast the hand that pushed my breast away.
Stunned, you will hear only silence.

So that later, with an indifferent smile, you'd say,
"My woman grows tame."

Not for a day—for centuries
I draw you to my chest, the monk's

Hand, cold until burning,
The hand—O Heloise!—of Abelard.

In the cathedral—to whip me to death—
You, whip soaring up like white lighting!

M.T. *(1920)*

Teeth, bright in her sleep,
silence, accurate in her eyes,
awakened without recall;
bland limbs of darkness
coil round her sleeping flesh,
its skin numb, cold,
like a husband's voice
requesting an answer
from silence, his wife.

                              N.K.

ORPHEUS

So they drifted: the lyre and the head,
Downstream, towards the endless stretch.
And the lyre sighed: "I will miss..."
And the lips completed: "the world..."

Shedding the silver-red trace,
The double trace in red silver,
In the swooning Hebrus—
My beloved brother! My sister!

At times, in unquenchable longing
The head slowed down.
But the lyre implored: "Float past!...."
And the lips responded: "Alas!"

Brought closer by the distant rippling,
Cradled as with a wedding wreath,
Is it the lyre shedding its blood?
Or the hair—its silver?

Descending the river's staircase
To the rippling pool of its cradle,
To that isle where the nightingale sings
His falsehoods better than ever...

Where are these hallowed remains?
Answer to this, salt water!
Has a bare-headed Lesbos girl
Perhaps caught them in her net?

M.T. (1921)

50

ORPHEUS

He sings his way up to being,
quietly, with unhurried breath,
as though words were a blossoming staircase
leading to a perfect sky
where the kind-eyed gods themselves
with slow, sinuous movements,
and ancient, immaculate hands
would greet him kindly: "Friend!"
As though the net to catch human souls
was masterfully spun of poetry,
of nothing but the sound of words,
not even the sense, the sound...
Where now are the moonlit woods
that stood up dark and strict
in the soft, thick mist of his longing,
now that he has constructed his perfect staircase
and burst through his silent sky?

N.K.

God

III

You will not tie him down
To your weights and signs!
Like the slenderest gymnast—
Through the tiniest chink...

God is fleeing us
With the migratory flights,
With the drawbridges,
And the telephone poles.

You will not train him
In fate and distress!
In the sedentary slush of feelings
He is a gray-haired ice-drift!

You will not overtake him!
In a domestic flowerpot
God does not sprout leaves
Like a tame begonia!

Under the vaulted dome,
All of them—poets and pilots—
Waited for the voice and the builder.
Hopelessness embraced them all.

For he is the speed—ever running.
For the infinite book of the stars—
From A to Z—
Is but a trace of his cloak!

M.T. (1922)

1.

If you ask what is God,
the answer is simple,
for each soul is a bird
not in the hand of a body
but in a hand of a tree,
count the birds
if you wish to know God,
for each soul is
a child of a tree,
each tree—
a child of the earth,
each earth—
a child of the sky,
each sky—
a child of the soul,
each soul—
a child of death,
each death—
a child of the earth.
Once you know this,
you won't ask what is God.
Now you know.

N.K.

2.

Lost, found,
lost again, caught again,
here it is, look at it,
its feet bound with rope,
this bird you searched for
on a tree you planted

(some call it the oblivion tree),
how many summers,
how many winters and springs
will it fly from you,
this bird with colorful feathers
(some call it the bird of happiness,
some call it God)
whose feet you bound with rope,
whose wings you cut,
whose nature is to fly
from anyone, anywhere,
from anything, anyone,
be it a person or a tree,
that wants it to stay forever?

N.K.

*
**

1.

Sweetly-sweetly, thinly-thinly
Something whistled in the pine.
In my dream I saw a baby
With midnight-colored eyes.

Still, hot resin keeps dripping
From the little scarlet pine.
Sawed apart, my heart is ripping
In this splendid night all mine.

M.T. (1916)

2.

SIBYL – TO THE NEWBORN

Cling to my breast,
Infant:
Birth is the fall into   days.

From the cloudy nowhere cliffs
How low
My infant fell.
You were a spirit, you became dust.

Cry, little one, for them and for us:
Birth is the fall into   hours.

Cry, little one, again, anew:
Birth is the fall into blood,
Into   dust,
Into   time...

Where is his miracles' splendor?
Cry, little one: birth into weight;

Into   blood,
Into   sweat...

You shall rise yet! What they call death
In the world—is the fall into heaven.

You shall see yet! What they call closed eyes
In the world—is the fall into light.

From now
Into forever.

Death, little one: not to sleep, but to rise,
Not to sleep, but to return.

Swim, little one! One staircase step
Behind you...
        —The ascent into day.

                                             M.T. (1923)

Small hands,
puffy cheeks,
tiny feet,
where did you go?

Small hands
clinging to me,
small mouth
opening,
small mouth
crying
"Mama! Mama!"

Little feet, little toes,
training shoes,
first dresses
tiny hats with sparkles,
tiny hats with flowers,
where did you go?

Little child
that kept me up all night,
little child,
where did you go?
That's life, they say,
what can you do,
children grow.

But I will repeat
until the day I die,
"Tiny hands,
tiny feet,
where did you go?"

N.K.

THE SIBYL

The Sibyl: burnt out; the sibyl: charred.
All the birds are dead but god is alive.

The sibyl: emptied out; the sibyl: a drought.
All veins have withered: the jealous groom.

The sibyl: dropped out; the sibyl: the crater
Of fate and destruction—the tree among maids.

Like a regal tree in the naked woods—
At first, the fire howled just like a tree.

Then, from under its lids—taking off, unaware,
Like rivers gone dry, the god took flight.

He sensed the waste of an outside search,
And his voice and his heart fell into me.

The sibyl: the oracle; the sibyl: the vault.
Thus, Annunciation came true in that exact

Unaging hour; thus, in gray-haired grass
Her mortal maidenhood became the cave

For the marvelous voice...
                    thus, becoming a starstorm—
The sibyl: dropped out of life.

M.T. (1922)

SIBYL

The sibyl
hides from the curious

(the water knows what equals it:
fire—earth—air);

a myth giving shape to history,
you

who could foretell everything
except your own end,

or the age at which
it would overtake you;

no longer Apollo's oracle,
a mere mortal,

you who have sloughed off ten skins,
thrown them to the wind

and ether;
you're now nothing but the voice,

the sound,
(like echo,

without a body:
god's greed for a mirror)

how you weep,
mother to Memory,
mere leaf, turmoil,
the muse's nurse,

your madness turned to
prophetic gift,

piping.

                                        N.K.

You will have your proof—wait!—
That, thrown out into the hay,
She needed neither glory, nor
Solomon's treasury.

No, wringing her hands behind her head,
—With a nightingale's throat!
Shulamith begs not for the treasury
But for a handful of red clay.

M.T. (1922)

Blot out this beauty
without strength
without a vestige of selflessness;
better to live without a tenth
of it than with seeming helplessness.

Better to live with a clear end
than to die into one end only,
like a yellow fruit an old love sent
dies instantly.

N.K.

I am paper to your pen;
I accept it all. I am a white page,
I am a keeper of your goods.
I will return it all, return it hundredfold.

I am country: I am black soil.
You are to me, rain and a ray.
You are my Lord and Master, while I am
White paper and black earth.

M.T. (1918)

Light,
light of my life,
exempt from thinking,
let me go out
neither with bang nor whimper,
but with a poem
whispering its way
from my heart to my lips,
and from my lips to a pencil,
and from the pencil—to paper,
and from paper—to the hearts of my friends!

N.K.

Do not call out to her:
Your call is a whiplash to her; your hail,
Like a haft-deep wound.
She is stirred down to her organ

Depths: the creative dread
Of intrusion; fear her: from her heights
(All fortresses stand upon chasms)
She might yet sing like an organ.

Will you withstand it? The mountain is
Steel and basalt; but, like an avalanche in the azure,
She will sing out with the full voice of the storm
In response to your seraph's alto.

It will come true! Fear it! A fall
Into the last hundredth! Hear!
—I retaliate for the singer's guttural call
With the organ tempest.

M.T. (1923)

Anything but the barren days,
the muse's smile of cold displeasure,
her love, steady yet apathetic,
a host of beings at her side
injecting tedium into self and nature.
Anything but the thought
—keep it out of consciousness—
formless thought, grown by night
into the self's body,
heavy and apathetic to the highest degree,
like an invalid melody.

N.K.

HAMLET'S DIALOGUE WITH HIS CONSCIENCE

She lies on the bottom, with silt
And weeds... She went there
To sleep—but even there sleep escapes her.
        —But I loved her
More than forty thousand brothers!
        —Hamlet!

She lies on the bottom, with silt.
Silt! And her last petal
Is awash on a log in the stream.
        —But I loved her
More than forty thousand...
        —Less though,
Than one lover.

She lies on the bottom, with silt.
—But did I
        (bewildered)
                love her?

M.T. (1923)

64

OPHELIA

If I'm neither blind nor deaf
nor purple nor blue nor orange,
then why does the camouflage work so well
and I become the color of leaves and flowers?
If I didn't lose my mind like Ophelia,
then what am I doing in this stream
floating on my back, flowers on both sides of me,
purple and orange and blue,
and no one can see me for what I am?
Or maybe those who can't see me are blind and deaf,
if, instead of a dying ocean, they see profits,
if, instead of the dying earth, they see only oil and gas?

N.K.

TO GENIUS

They christened us in the same tub,
They wed us with the same wreath,
They tortured us in the same jail,
They branded us with the same iron.

They will build us the same house.
They will cover us with the same mound.

M.T. (1918)

Learn to live
without flesh

learn to walk
without legs

learn to see
without eyes

learn to breathe
without air

get used to death
before it's here

N.K.

Along the large quiet roads,
With large quiet steps...
The soul is like a stone thrown into water—
Its circles ever widening...

Deep is that water, dark is that water...
The soul forever buried in the chest...
And I so want to take it out of there,
And I so want to tell it: Come into me!

M.T. (1920)

See your image
steeped in my shadow
change, yet resemble you,
tighten its fingers
around my soul
faltering, yet staying,
disguised, yet true.
Fingers unwrithing,
limp on my gown:
seeing is finding
but upside down.

N.K.

SISTER

Hell and Heaven are not enough:
They are already dying for you.

Following the brother into his fire—
Is it customary? Not a place for
Sisterly love, but for the flame-red passion.
With the brother, under the burial mound...
Is it customary?
                    —He was mine and will be! Even if rotted away!

This is the grave's supremacy!

M.T. (1923)

What can death do to me
that it hasn't done yet?
What can it take
that hasn't been taken?
it can only lift
what hasn't been lifted,
it can only unfold
what has been folded
by what calls itself life
yet is not alive;
it folded itself onto me,
until every breath became war.
I do not lie
when I say
there's death
in every breath,
(and a common rhyme it is, too!).
Think "дух" and "дыхание",*
"anima" and "animal",
then turn them upside down:
now you get it.
So hello there, silly old Mr. Death,
and how do you do?

N.K.

*"дух" (Russian for spirit) has the same root as "дыхание"
(Russian for "breath" or "breathing").

Perhaps, the best victory
Over time and gravity
Is to pass without a trace,
Without having even cast a shadow

On the walls...
                    To reject it all
Perhaps, to erase one's image from the mirrors;
Like Lermontov in the Caucasus,
To steal by without stirring up the rocks?

Perhaps, it would have been droll
Not to have touched the organ echo
With the finger of Sebastian Bach;
To dissolve, without having left dust

For the urn?
                    Perhaps, to lie
One's way out; to get discharged from latitudes;
To steal through Time as through an
Ocean, its waters left unstirred...

M.T. (1923)

The lesser magic,
the greater unknown,
a shadowy host,
the immortal dust,
what's this life about
but letting go,
enough time for the mouth
to unlearn the word "mine",
enough time for the bone
to grow old and weak,
enough time for the mind
to forget the names
of all who are gone;
what's immortality,
but the lesser magic,
the greater unknown,
mold on the host,
dust on a gravestone.

N.K.

THE CREVASSE

Neither friendship nor love will know
How this history ended.
Each day your answer is more muffled,
Each day you are sinking deeper.

No longer ruffled by anything—
Only a tree branch swaying—
Fallen into a glacial crevasse:
This breast that has crushed against you so!

Out of the storehouse of semblances
Pick out—at random—your augury:
You sleep in me as in a crystal
Coffin, you sleep in me

As in a deep wound—the crevasse is tight!
The glacier, jealous of its dead:
A ring, a shield, a seal, a belt,
Without return and without answer.

Widows, you curse Helen needlessly!
It's not in the fire of Helen's
Red Troy!—but in the blue of the glacial
Crevasse at whose bottom you sleep...

Having mated with you like Aetna
With Empedocles... Fall asleep, dreamer!
And tell your family it is all in vain:
This breast does not relinquish its dead.

M.T. (1923)

AWAKE IN ME

Awake in me, you sleep
the sleep of knowing—
memory is silence
hungry for music,
self is the world
hungry for a face,
seed is a stone
hungry for living,
and every paradox in the world
ends in death.

Awake in me, you know
the knowledge of sleep—
words are a trap
set by the mouth,
body is memory
disfigured by light,

poems are bird language
calling
—like every paradox in the world—
for silence.

N.K.

SAHARA

Do not search, handsome lads!
Stifling him with sands,
The soul won't tell
Of him who is missing.

You search in vain, handsome
Lads—I'm telling the truth!
He who is missing rests
In a safe coffin.

With his poems like lands
Of miracles and fire,
With his poems like countries
He rode into me:

Arid and sandy,
Fathomless, dayless.
With his poems like lands
He vanished in me.

Listen, without jealousy,
To this story of souls.
The sandy drought—
Into the oasis of eyes...

The beseeching throb
Of the Adam's apple...
I grasped him death-tight,
Like passion and God.

Nameless, he vanished!
Won't be found. Taken.
Deserts have no memory—
Thousands sleep in them.

The upwelling waves

Quieting down as foam.
Buried under the sand:
The Sahara is your mount.

M.T. *(1923)*

I will grow myself quiet leaves
in the difficult silence of chastity.

I will hide in the immense namelessness
though each tree murmurs to him my name.

I am the bed of leaves he can never scorch,
not even with his eyes of fire.

I am the naked face of the flower; a cross.
He cannot escape by reaching me.

The god and the goal; the lover and the loved;
the pursuit and the flight, entwined.

Though a god, he will die in the depths of my bark.
I will glisten his face on my leaves.

Every eagle will have his eyelids.
Every event—his speed.

Each one of the thousand suns
will pursue me as he has chased.

Each one of the symbols of silence
will learn his name I refuse to bear.

I am he: the sun, its immense bowl
pouring out selves as from a fount of chastity.

He is I: the ever-green song in flight,
the sun forever pursuing me.

N.K.

The hour when the kings on high
Bear gifts each to each
(The hour I descend the mountain)
The mountain begins to see.

Plots densely crowd the circle.
Fates draw together: no escape.
The hour I don't see my hands:

The souls begin to see.

M.T. (1923)

Faithful to the more or less imperfect sounds,
a silent man becomes a symbol for the voiceless world
that drowns out speech, just as it drowns out fire
of thought, just as it drowns out thought;
while only one form is left, numb and maternal,
a voiceless, blind clutter—feelings' maze:
the soul's need for solitude: the self of cravings
dissolved in silence.

N.K.

I love you, but the torment is still alive.
Find the lullaby words to soothe it.
Rainy words, words that are spendthrift.
Make them up yourself; so that, in their leaves,

Rain dribbles: not a flail thrashing grain:
Rain drumming the roof: streaming down my brow,

Down my coffin, so that my coffin lit up,
My fever calmed, somebody slept

On and on...
        They say that water
Seeps through the chinks—People
Lie in rows, without a moan, waiting
For the unknown. (They will burn—me.)

Rock me to sleep, but I ask of you:
Not with letters—with the shelter of your hands,

With softness...

                                            M.T. (1923)

If I am a fruit of oblivion,
then are you my memory's tree?

If I flap my wings of a soul,
then do you flap yours—of a mind?

If I am a pebble of a time-river,
then are you a rock of time?

If you are my memory's tree,
then watch that I don't fall.

                                            N.K.

In the inmost hour of the soul,
In the inmost hour—of the night...
(The gigantic stride of the soul,
Of the soul in the night)

In that hour, soul, reign
Over the worlds you desire.
To rule is the lot of the soul:
Soul, reign.

Cover lips with rust; snow lightly
Upon the lashes...
(The Atlantic sigh of the soul,
Of the soul in the night...)

In that hour, soul, darken
The eyes in which you will rise
Like Vega... make bitter
The sweetest fruit, soul.

Make bitter: darken:
Grow: reign.

                                        M.T. *(1923)*

TIME OF RETURN

I'm a backward
sound of myself.
I twist, I turn

through sheer virulence
of habit sleep
that measures time

in bursts of agony.
I ask, I bless.
I speak the raw material of memory:

only flowers here still recall the dead.
This is the hour of the soul.
I am a green begonia,

a red petal
on the stem of morning.
Sweet hour of return,

save me from these shattered
words, repetitive illusions.
I am dark, uncountable.

I am the meaning of a syllable
the ancients said and dropped.
I am the one the clouds dream of

when their vapor eyes are shut.
The weeping wall, the nakedness of heart...
Disinterestedness, now let me go.

You said: it's guaranteed—
the backward glance, the exit,
the twisting back, back, back...

Now let me go, beauty grass.
Your kisses pain me
as all that dies pains that which doesn't.

I am the eye-nerve of your marriage,
grassy sky.
I ask, I bless.

I am a friend to everything that's mortal.
I beg you: do breathe me in
and let me disappear in you:

Forever, earth.
Forever, sky.

N.K.

I am. You shall be. Between us—a chasm.
I drink. You thirst. All talk is futile.
Ten years—a hundred thousand years
Part us. God does not build bridges.
Be—This is my commandment. Let me pass
And not disturb your growth with my breathing.
I am. You shall be. In ten years' time
You'll say: I am—I will say: I was.

M.T. *(1918)*

The one who is set apart
who hasn't been born yet
whose birth is a ship
unmoored
unanchored
unmarked
waiting to sail in an open sea
death awaits in the shallows
death awaits in the deeps
death surrounds the unborn
as the sea swallows the ship

N.K.

BEYOND SIGHT

Reciprocity, do not obstruct
The Castalian flow.
Nonpresence: the greater substance
Lying beyond the eye.

Beyond speech, beyond sight,
Like a prolonged la note
Stretching out miles of distance
Between the temptation and the lips.

Blessed are the longitudes,
The latitudes of Lethe and zones!
Furthering into you with distance
As with the whole note; stretching out

Into you like a moan;
Striking against you like an echo
Into the chest of granite:
Do not see, do not hear, do not exist—

I've no need for white
Upon black—the chalk of the blackboard!
Nearly beyond the confines
Of soul, beyond the limits of pain—

The last card of my verbal arrogance
Has been dealt.
Distance, you are now nothing but
A blank wall to me.

M.T. (1923)

Be in me as a voiceless song
    that never ceases, and not
As spoken words are—
    arrogant and gaudy.
Hide me in an artless language
    of sleeping truths
in an unscattered mind.
    Let the unsaid shield us
amid tinsel phrases.
    Poised rocks of silence,
Keep us.

N.K.

MINUTE

Minute: the disappearing one: you will pass.
Pass me by then, passion and friendship!
What tomorrow would tear away from my hands
I throw out today!

Minute: the measuring one! Cheating
On the most minute detail! Listen:
That which ended—
Never began. Lie then, flatter

Others, still subject to the measles
Of fraction, still not grown out of
Deeds. Who are you to squander
Away the sea? The watershed

Of a living soul? O trinket? O trifle!
The glorious King of Bounties
Had no kingdom worthier than
The legend on his ring: "This, too,

Shall pass..." On their roads back
Who did not plumb the vanity
Of your clock-faced Arabias,
Of your pendulums' toil?

Minute: the torment! The racing illusion:
Still lingering! Grinding us
Into trash and ashes! You that will pass:
Minute: charity to the dogs.

O how I long to leave the world
Where pendulums rend the soul,
Where the succession of minutes
Rules my eternity.

M.T. (1923)

84

He stunned himself,
he solved every single riddle.
A ghost came up to him,
"Are you my friend?"
he asked the ghost,
the ghost's response was "No".
"O just as well," he smiled to himself,
"A friend is neither here nor there."
When a strong wind gathered,
the ghost swayed in the wind,
the papers circled round him.
Ah, said the man, how I love thee,
he said again, still stunned,
now that you blew away my answers,
what keeps me here? Nothing.
Take everything—my arms, my legs...
Free me from this sickly body.
"No," said the ghost strictly, "Live."

N.K.

You who loved me with the falsehood
Of truth—and with the truth of falsehood;
Who loved me to the limits
Of the possible—beyond all limits—

You who loved me longer
Than Time—one sweep of an arm!
You no longer love me:
These five words are the truth.

M.T. (1923)

Only what shatters you
lets you live:
a love that breaks you,
a child's birth
that doesn't break you completely,
or a death of a part of your soul
unduly attached to another—
all of this lets you live unencumbered,
free of all earthly burdens,
free of everything—that is, of every thing,
except the body,
but this, too, you'll be free of one fine day.

N.K.

(from "Poem of the End")

Wouldn't it be a hundred times better
To become the Wandering Jew?
For anyone not scum,
Life is a pogrom.

Life loves only converts,
Judases of all faiths!
Go to a leper colony! To hell!
Anywhere, but not into life,

It spares only traitors,
Sheep for the butcher!
My birth certificate
I trample underfoot!

I trample it! Vengeance:
David's shield avenged. Into the crush of bodies.
Isn't it thrilling that the yid
Did not want to live?

M.T. (Prague, 1 February 1924 – Ilovisci, 8 June 1924)

silver hair yellow stars
gold teeth children's shoes
this church of memory
hides the temple of all beginnings
we shall walk to our graves
remembering them

N.K.

AN ISLAND

There is an island—snatched away from the Nereids
With an underground shock;
A virgin, tracked down
By no one: undiscovered.

It overflows with fern. It hides in sea
Foam. The route? The fare?
I know only: it is listed
Nowhere except in your Columbus's

Eyes. Two palm trees
So clearly seen!... Gone. A condor's
Wing flapping...
        (Enough about your
Islands!—in a sleeping car!)

One hour, or perhaps a week
Of sailing (a year—if I insist!)
I know only: it is listed
nowhere except in latitudes

 Of the future ...

M.T. (1924)

BARE ROCK

How far I had to walk
just to be near you,
bare rock,
all that's left of the empire
that once ruled the seas,
not to mention the earth,
the entire world known to men
of the past which is now a shadow
known only to lovers of myth,
as well as to ordinary lovers,
to whom you appear in a dream,
as you twice appeared to me,
bare rock.

N.K.

There are rhymes in this world.
Disjoin them, and it trembles.
You were a blind man, Homer.
Night sat on your eyebrows.

Night, your singer's cloak.
Night, on your eyes, like a shutter.
Would a seeing man not have joined
Achilles to Helen?

Helen. Achilles.
Name a better sounding match.
For, in defiance of chaos,
The world thrives on accords.

You were a blind man, bard.
You littered fortune like trash.
Those rhymes have been forged in that
World, and as you draw them apart

This world crumbles. Who needs
An accord! Grow old, Helen!
Achaia's best warrior!
Sparta's sweet beauty!

Nothing, but the murmur
Of myrtle, a lyre's dream:
"Helen. Achilles.
The couple kept apart."

M.T. (1924)

HELEN REENVISIONS HER LIFE

This highly unstable love
would appreciate fruitful hearth,
fire stoked by a husband's hand,
dark cakes rising fat in the oven;
years of sameness on a quiet hill,
amid empty lots and inelegant housing;
a staunch cabin withstanding time
even while thoughts change like clouds.
Silence kept fresh in an ancient jar;
the sky unbleached and a wife's vision fair,
while the wind brings young trees into motion.

N.K.

Thus—only Helen looks past the Trojan
Roofs. In the stupor of her eyes
Four provinces left bloodless
And a hundred centuries forlorn.

Thus—only Helen, towering above marital strife,
Thinks: my nudity
Has left four Arabias frozen
And five seas drained of pearls.

Thus only Helen—do not expect to see
Her wringing her hands!—wonders at this host
Of crown princes left homeless
And chieftains rushing to fight.

Thus only Helen—do not expect to see
Her pleading lips!—wonders at this ditch
Heaped up with princes:
At the sonlessness of a hundred tribes.

But no, not Helen! Not that bigamous
Thief, the pestilential draught.
What treasury have you squandered
That you now look into our eyes as

Even Helen at the great supper
Did not dare—into the eyes of her slaves:
Gods. "The land left husbandless by an outsider
Still, like a caterpillar, groveling towards her feet."

M.T. (1924)

SHADOW OVER THE TOWN

Helen's shadow on Trojan rocks
still threatens the Greeks,
burdens them with the highest taxes
the loved exacts from the lover:
middle-class teashop warmth forsaken,
adding machines count the killed,
a scarce spring, a fruitless autumn,
quiet markets and barren cribs:
see the wretched pass for the mad,
the mad for the licentious
shadows creeping after the main
shadow over the town—
the feared outlines of the woman
washed clean of mercy,
memory of guilt reflecting
future centuries' blood.

N.K.

Squeezed with the hollows
Of existence, in a stupor of backwoods,
Buried alive under the avalanche
Of days, I serve my sentence in life.

My tomb-like, forsaken wintering.
Death: frost on my red lips—
No health other than this
I ask from God and from spring.

M.T. *(1925)*

When it finally comes,
it will not say "Now!",
nor will it raise a scythe
in its skeletal hands,
or a black flag with, say,
skull and crossbones,
it's not a pirate ship, after all.
If it feels like talking at all,
it'll say only "Oops, I'm late,
I know you expected me,
I got held up with another fool,
who didn't recognize me
and refused to follow orders."
No, not even that.
It'll say nothing at all.
It'll be dressed as a nurse at Mt. Sinai*
bending over my still body
to torment me with yet another shot.
So let it come,
since it will come anyway
with or without a scythe
(just another word for a syringe),
injections, pills, crossbones.
Speed is all that matters
in matters of leave-taking.
Make it quick,
don't drag it out
for another twenty or thirty years,
and not in a hospital bed
but on top of a craggy hill,
with the smell of the sea in my nostrils,
the salt, the breeze, land's end.

N.K.

* Mt. Sinai – a hospital in New York

My veins slashed open: unrestrained,
Unrestorable, my life gushes forth.
Hold steady your plates and your bowls!
Each bowl soon will be shallow,
The plates—too flat to contain it.
                    Up the brim and over
Staining earth dark, nourishing weeds.
Irreversible, unavoidable,
Unrestorable, the poem streams.

M.T. (1934)

See how nothing
keeps out of Pluto's gorge,
silently drifts
towards it, waits, sinks
into the thickening dark,
the unreflecting water,
grave made of mud and stones:
this way—to hide lizard shadows,
that way—to rob of flesh.
Although mercy's an unprofitable profession,
save me from too much death.

N.K.

Nina Kossman is a Moscow-born poet, painter, sculptor, bilingual writer, translator of Russian poetry, and playwright. Her English short stories and poems have been published in US, Canadian, British, and Dutch journals. Her Russian prose and poems have been published in major Russian literary journals. Among her published books are two books of poems in Russian and English as well as two volumes of translations of Marina Tsvetaeva's poems. Her other books include *Behind the Border* (HarperCollins, 1994), a collection of stories about her Moscow childhood; *Gods and Mortals: Modern Poems on Classical Myths* (Oxford University Press anthology, 2001); a bilingual collection of short stories about her teaching; and a novel originally published in English, later translated into Russian. She lives in New York.

Marina Tsvetaeva is one of Russia's greatest 20th century poets. Born in Moscow in 1892, she came into artistic maturity at the outset of the Russian revolution. She followed her husband into exile in 1922, thus most of her great work was written in the West – first in Berlin, then in Prague, and finally in Paris. When she returned to the Soviet Union in 1939, her husband was arrested as an "enemy of the people" and shot, her daughter was arrested, too. Tsvetaeva took her own life in Elabuga, a small town in the Republic of Tatarstan, shortly after she had been evacuated from Moscow following the Nazi invasion of the Soviet Union, in 1941.

CPSIA information can be obtained
at www.ICGtesting.com
Printed in the USA
LVHW021530050322
712646LV00017B/2002

9 780999 073742